T0090775

Faith *for* Today

Jerry R Griffith Jr

WESTBOW
P R E S S®
A DIVISION OF THOMAS NELSON
& ZONDERVAN

Scripture quotations from The Authorized (King James)
Version. Rights in the Authorized Version in the United
Kingdom are vested in the Crown. Reproduced by permission
of the Crown's patentee, Cambridge University Press

WestBow Press books may be ordered through booksellers or by contacting:

WestBow Press
A Division of Thomas Nelson & Zondervan
1663 Liberty Drive
Bloomington, IN 47403
www.westbowpress.com
1 (866) 928-1240

ISBN: 978-1-9736-1775-4 (sc)
ISBN: 978-1-9736-1774-7 (e)

Print information available on the last page.

WestBow Press rev. date: 02/05/2018

Contents

The Bible

The word Bible comes from a Latin word which means the book. The Bible or the Book is God's written revelation of himself to mankind. The central theme of the Bible is God's son, Jesus Christ.

The Bible contains 66 books or divisions, written by 40 authors over about 1600 years. It is divided into 2 sections, 39 Books of the Old Testament and 27 Books of the New Testament.

The Old Testament or old covenant is the agreement God made with mankind about his relationship to God before the coming of Jesus. The New Testament, or new covenant, is the agreement God made with man about his relationship with God after the coming of Jesus Christ.

The Bible tells us God's plan for mankind from the creation until the end of time. It teaches us God's standards of right and wrong, tells us how to make peace with God, and gives us practical wisdom and principles for daily living.

The Bible is the only book that claims to be the inspired word of God and is the only book that will endure forever.

GENESIS

Genesis is the title given to the first book of the Bible. Genesis means origin or beginning, and the book tells us the beginning of life and of God's plan for the human race. Genesis also records major events such as the great flood, which have affected the rest of history.

In Genesis, Moses recorded the beginning of created life, including the creation of man. He also recorded the beginning of sin, and God's divine plan for bringing sinful man back to God.

Genesis also gives us the beginning of family life, languages, races, government and nations. One specially chosen nation, Israel, which began as a group of Hebrew slaves in Egypt, who will be used in carrying out God's plan for man thru the rest of the Bible.

Genesis tells of outstanding people such as Noah and Abraham who believed God under difficult circumstances. Their experience of faith helps us to have greater confidence in all of God's promises today.

Genesis is an exciting book and gives us the foundation for the rest of God's word.

Exodus

Exodus is the name given to the second Book of the Bible and tells of God's deliverance of his people from slavery in Egypt. The word Exodus means going out or leaving, and is an exciting demonstration of God's power as he sets his people free.

Exodus also shows God's concern and provision for his people, from the miraculous crossing of the Red Sea to the end of 40 years of wondering in the wilderness. During this time God provided food that fell from the sky, clothes that never wore out, and water from a rock in the desert. He also led the people by a cloud in the day and a pillar of fire at night. The Exodus shows us what God can do for his people today.

Exodus also records the giving of God's civil, ceremonial, and moral law. These laws are summarized in what we call the 10 commandments. These laws of God make us aware of man's sinful nature, and show us that man is in need of a savior to deliver him from the bondage of sin.

The Exodus also gives us a greater appreciation for the death of Jesus Christ, who fulfilled the law's demand that sin be punished when he died on the cross for our sins.

LEVITICUS

Leviticus is the title of the third book of the Bible and was written by Moses. The title refers to the Levites or Priests of God who were the descendents of the tribe of Levi in the nation of Israel.

Leviticus was written to show the people how to approach God and to live in fellowship with God through a system of sacrifices, and by being separated from the world.

God directed his people to build a tabernacle or portable tent, where he could meet with them. Great detail is given to the instructions for offering sacrifices and for the office of the priest, who would approach God in the tabernacle on behalf of the people. These offerings give us a picture of Christ's great sacrifices when he died on the cross.

In Exodus God spoke to his people from his presence on the mountain, while in Leviticus he speaks to his people from his presence in the tabernacle. Leviticus reminds us that God's dwelling place is now in the heart of each person who receives his son Jesus Christ and therefore, there is no need of further sacrifices in order to approach God.

NUMBERS

The fourth book of the Bible is called Numbers and was written by Moses. It is so named because the people of Israel were counted or numbered two times. This book of Numbers also contains the history of Israel as the people traveled from the Red Sea to the promised land of Canaan.

Numbers records two generations of people over a time of 40 years and shows God leading them to their destination.

The first generation of Israel reached the Promised Land after about two years. The people did not believe God when he said he would help them conquer the land, so they rebelled and went back into the wilderness for another 38 years. During this time they hardened their hearts against God so that he said they would die, and the next generation would go into the land. Even Moses would not be permitted to enter the land because of his sin of hitting the rock instead of speaking to it as God had instructed him.

The children or next generation of Israel were again counted and given some further instructions as they approached the land of Canaan a second time.

Numbers reminds us of the danger of letting sin harden our hearts so that we no longer believe God's word. We must be careful that we don't miss the place God has promised to us, called Heaven.

DEUTERONOMY

In the fifth book of the Bible, called Deuteronomy, God's people finally reached their destination because of the faithfulness of God. This book gets its name from 2 words which mean second law. God was not giving a second set of law's but was giving the Law of Moses again to the new generation of Israel before they entered the Promised Land.

Deuteronomy shows us the importance of one generation passing on God's word to the next. It also reminds us of the need to review God's word again and again.

As God was faithful to lead his people thru the wilderness and supply their needs for 40 years, he now gives them a second chance to occupy Canaan. We can be encouraged by knowing that God is a God of a second chance.

We may fail in life, rebel and sin against God, but again call on God and ask for another chance. This book also reminds us that we must give the word of God to the next generation so that they won't forget the God of the word.

JOSHUA

In the Old Testament, the Book of Joshua is the story of the new leader of Israel who took the people into the Promised Land after the death of Moses. The name Joshua means Jehovah is salvation.

In this book God's great power is seen by Israel as God parted the water of the flooded Jordan River to let his people cross over on dry land. The first battle they fought after crossing Jordan was at the famous city of Jericho.

The great victory at Jericho shows us what God can do for his people when they follow his instructions completely. The tragic defeat at the next little town of Ai shows how helpless man is when God's blessing is withheld because of man's sin.

The central theme of Joshua is that victory comes from faithful obedience of God's word. We can face the difficult, heart-breaking trials of life without undue fear when we know we are on God's side. As Joshua said to the people, (*) "choose you this day whom you will serve, but as for me and my house, we will serve the Lord."

(*) Josh. 24:15

JUDGES

The Old Testament Book of Judges continues the history of Israel after the death of Joshua. During this time God raised up leaders called Judges who delivered the people from serving other nations.

This book tells of 13 Judges who delivered Israel from periods of punishment after the people had rebelled and sinned against God. In this we see the constant sinfulness and failure of man, but we also see the constant love and mercy of God in restoring his people.

Some of the best known Judges are Gideon, who defeated a large army with just 300 soldiers, and Samson, who had unusual physical strength because of his vow to God.

The book of the Judges is an illustration of the lives of many people today who are unhappy or suffering as a result of their sinful living. It also reminds us that if we find ourselves in such circumstances, we can call on God and ask for forgiveness and help, knowing that he is a God of mercy who can restore his people to victorious living.

RUTH

The Old Testament Book of Ruth took place during the time of the Judges of Israel and is named after the central person in the story. This is a love story about a virtuous woman who becomes the great-grandmother of King David.

The story of Ruth illustrates the theme of the kinsman redeemer which was a law of the land in those days.

Ruth, who was from the land of Moab, chose to follow her mother-in-law to the land of Israel after the death of her first husband, saying, (*) "thy people shall be my people and thy God my God".

After arriving in Israel, Ruth met Boaz, a relative of her deceased husband. Boaz had a right to redeem or buy his relatives inheritance including the right to marry the widow Ruth. He not only had the right, but was able to pay the price and was willing to do so.

This story of the kinsman redeemer is an illustration of Jesus Christ. He became our kinsman when he came to earth as a member of the human race. Jesus was able to pay the price to redeem or buy us from sin, and he proved that he was willing to do so when he died on the cross.

(*) Ruth 1:16

1 SAMUEL

The Old Testament Book of 1 Samuel records a part of the history of Israel covering about 115 years from the birth of Samuel, who was the last of the judges of Israel, to the death of Saul, who was the first of the kings.

The main three characters of this book are Judge Samuel, King Saul, and young David, the shepherd who would become the next king. During this time the people rejected God's leadership, and wanted a king over them like the other nations around them. God permitted Israel to have a king, even though it would cause them much suffering in the future.

Soon after Saul became the first king, he began to rebel against God by being impatient, being jealous of David who had killed the giant Goliath, and by turning to witchcraft. Saul finally ended his own life by falling on his sword when his army was being defeated.

1 Samuel is a tragic illustration of what happens when God's people want to be like the rest of the world. We must remember that in order to have God's blessing on us, we must follow his instructions for daily living and not be conformed to the world.

2 SAMUEL

The Old Testament Book of 2 Samuel contains the history of Israel while David was king. This book tells of David's great triumphs which began when he was at Hebron for seven years. He then united all of Israel into one kingdom and moved the capital to Jerusalem where he reigned for another 33 years. During this time David was successful on all sides and God made a covenant with David that his family would continue on the throne forever.

However, this book also tells of David's great tragedies. Instead of going to battle with the army, David remained in Jerusalem. This led to his sin with Bathsheba, resulting in the murder of her husband. God was displeased with David's sins, and the prophet Nathan told him that he would suffer the consequences of his sin so long as he lived.

Although God forgave David, and used him to write scriptures, David had trouble all his life. This book teaches us that God will forgive us, even if our sins are as severe as David's, but we may have to suffer the consequences in this life.

2 Samuel also gives us hope that even though we have sinned, God can still use us in his service and restore the joy of our salvation by giving us a clean heart like he did for David.

1 KINGS

The Old Testament Book of 1 Kings continues the history of Israel during the time when Solomon was king. This son of David ruled for 40 years as Israel reached its peak of wealth and power. Solomon had the temple constructed, and Jerusalem became the religious as well as the political capital of Israel.

Although Solomon was the wisest man to ever live, and wrote many inspired proverbs, he did not follow God's word completely. He accumulated far to much gold and silver, had several thousand fine horses, and hundreds of wives. All three were in violation of God's standards for kings, and his wives eventually influenced him toward idol worship.

God warned Solomon that because of his sins, the kingdom would be divided after his death. Solomon's sons who succeeded him would not listen to wise advice of older men, and split the nation into Israel in the north and Judah in the south. The divided kingdoms were weakened, continued in idol worship, and were eventually conquered.

1 King reminds us that even though we may be very successful in life, disobeying God's word can lead to failure and destruction, while obeying his word will lead us to believing in his son Jesus Christ, and will give us practical instruction for daily living

2 KINGS

The Old Testament Book of 2 Kings gives us the history of Israel during the time the nation was divided into Israel in the north and Judah in the south. Israel had 19 kings and the nation lasted for 250 years, while Judah had 20 kings and lasted 390 years before being conquered.

God's people in both nations were influenced by the heathen and worshipped idols. Wickedness became very great and reached its peak under rulers such as King Ahab and Queen Jezebel. God sent prophets like Elijah to warn the people of approaching judgment, but they rejected the prophets and God's word.

2 Kings also records the many miracles that God did thru the prophets in order to convince the people to turn back to God.

This book reminds us today that it is dangerous to ignore God's warnings of judgment and continue in willful sin.

God's word tells us that just as the kings were held accountable for their actions, we too must give an account to God.

2 Kings also shows us that we must not be influenced by the evil of the world, but by the word of God.

1 & 2 CHRONICLES

The Old Testament Books of the Chronicles gives us the historical account of events in Israel during the time of the kings. The Chronicles review the family line back to Adam, and record some of the major events leading up to the great captivity in Babylon.

While the Books of Samuel and the Kings emphasize the throne of Israel, the Chronicles emphasize the temple of God. During this time the temple became a symbol of the unity of the Hebrew people. It was also a reminder of the high calling of God for the nation, and was a visible reminder that God was still with his people.

The Chronicles show us that a nation's response to God determines its history, as Israel's continuing in idol worship led to their destruction and captivity for 70 years.

As the temple was a symbol to Israel, the church is a symbol to God's people today. The church reminds us that God still has a purpose for his people, and that he will be with us until the end of time.

The Chronicles should also remind us that our response to God will determine the future of our nation. We must pray for those in authority so that we may live peaceful lives and have greater opportunity to tell the rest of the world the good news of Jesus Christ.

EZRA

The Old Testament Book of Ezra tells of the return of a remnant of God's people back to Jerusalem after the great captivity in Babylon, This great captivity which lasted for 70 years was the result of Israel's continuing to worship idols instead of God.

This return to the homeland had been predicted by Jeremiah and Isaiah even before the captivity began. Two groups of people were permitted to return, and Ezra was the leader of the second group.

Under the leadership of Ezra the new temple was built and dedicated to God. Ezra then used the word of God to lead the people to a revival of worship of God in the temple. This revival, or renewal, resulted in God's people separating themselves from the idol worshipping people around them. Israel has never again returned to idol worship since the time of Ezra.

The book of Ezra reminds us of our need to returning to a right relationship with Jesus Christ after we have sinned. Ezra shows us that hearing the word of God leads to genuine spiritual revival and dedication to the Lord, which results in separation from the evil of the world.

NEHEMIAH

The Old Testament Book of Nehemiah takes place after the remnant of God's people returned to Jerusalem to rebuild the temple and the city after the great captivity in Babylon.

Nehemiah had heard that the wall was not rebuilt around Jerusalem and therefore the city was without protection. Nehemiah was given permission from the Persian governor to go back to Jerusalem to build the wall and gate. Under his careful organization and leadership the wall was rebuilt in just seven weeks.

There was much opposition to this work from the enemies of God's people. They used ridicule, threats, false accusations, and attempted compromise to try to stop Nehemiah. However, he was determined to do God's work and would not stop long enough to argue with the enemies.

After the wall was completed the people recognized their need of spiritual revival and they asked Nehemiah to read the scriptures. After hearing the word of God, the people made a new covenant to live according to God's will.

Nehemiah is a great example of a leader who was determined to do God's will in spite of all opposition. The book is also a reminder to us that we must hear the word of God in order to know his will for our lives, and to have spiritual revival.

ESTHER

The Old Testament Book of Esther took place during the time of the great captivity in Babylon when many of the Hebrews chose to stay in the luxury of the Persian Empire rather than return to Jerusalem.

The name of God is never mentioned in this book, yet it is an example of God's care over his people even through they did not return to the homeland.

The main character of the book is Esther, a Jew who became a queen in the Persian Empire. When a jealous politician under the king succeeded in getting a death sentence passed on all the Jews, Esther risked her life to plead for her people before the king.

Her righteous uncle Mordecai reminded her that this may have been the reason why God allowed her to become queen.

The king was persuaded to send out another decree granting protection to all the Jews. This is a picture of God providing for our salvation through the death of Jesus Christ when we were all under the death sentence because of our sins.

This book also teaches us that God has a will for our lives and can use us in carrying out his plan for the salvation of mankind.

JOB

The Old Testament Book of Job is the first of the books of poetry and is believed to be the oldest book in the Bible. The first 17 books of the Bible are historical and deal with mankind and the nation of Israel. Job, however, is about an individual person and deals with the human heart.

We have all heard of "the patience of Job" and this book does tell of his patience while enduring suffering. Job did not know that God was allowing Satan to bring heartache and suffering into his life in order to see if Job would rebel and sin against God.

Job's wife turned against him and his friends began to accuse him of some great sin, for they believed that God would not allow a righteous man to suffer.

Through all his suffering, Job kept his faith in God saying, (*) "Though he slay me, yet will I trust in him". Job also believed in life after death saying that he would see God face to face.

In this story God spoke to Job out of a tornado reminding him that God is still far more powerful than man and that man does not understand all the workings of God

Job teaches us that godly righteous people do suffer in this life but reminds us that God is still in charge of the whole universe. If we suffer we can call on God for help knowing that he has not forsaken us.

(*) Job 13:15

PSALMS

The Old Testament Book of the Psalms is a collection of 150 Hebrew poems or songs of praise written mostly by David. The central message of the Psalms is, (*) "Praise ye the Lord". The Psalms tell of human experience, human feelings, and personal meditations about God.

There are several types of psalms including instructional, praise and thanksgiving, historical, confession of sin, prayers, psalms about Jesus Christ, and even psalms of anger asking for God's wrath on wicked people.

The Psalms were used as a prayer and praise book by the nation of Israel in their early temple worship. The Jews today use the Psalms in their synagogues. The early Christian Church sang the Psalms, while the various denominations of Christianity are still blessed by the Psalms today.

The Psalms help us put our feeling into words and give us various ways to express our praise for God. The Psalms also give us strength and comfort during difficult times such as death.

David's great Psalms of prayer confessing his sins to God remind us of God's love for us in spite of our sins. This prayer also shows us that God can redeem our broken lives and use us in his service.

People of all ages have been blessed by the words of the young shepherd who said, (**) "The Lord is my shepherd" and reminds us Jesus Christ will be our shepherd if we will receive him into our lives.

(*) Psa 150:1
(**) Psa 23:1

PROVERBS

The Old Testament Book of Proverbs is a collection of 917 wise sayings written and collected almost entirely by Solomon. These inspired wise sayings teach us God's wisdom instead of man's, and gives us practical advice for everyday living.

The central theme of Proverbs is that true wisdom begins with the proper fear or respect for God, and places great value on gaining knowledge and wisdom as we go thru life.

The Book of Proverbs also teaches the importance of proper values and character development beginning with early training for children.

If we want to avoid being conformed to this world's values and philosophies the Proverbs can help us be transformed or changed in our minds. If we want to be more like Christ then we must have the wisdom of God, especially in these times of religious confusion.

The world places great value on education, but the Proverbs remind us that learning without wisdom in not enough.

God's word shows us that his wisdom is far above man's, but we can gain wisdom from God by a careful study of his word.

ECCLESIASTES

The Old Testament Book of Ecclesiastes is about man's search for meaning in life. The title comes from the Latin form of a Greek word meaning "The Preacher". Solomon is the author and he records his own experience while out of fellowship with God.

The central message is that life that is lived for self without God is empty. Solomon sought satisfaction through pleasure, wealth, knowledge, a form of religion, and philosophy. He concluded that all these and the other things he pursued were vanity or emptiness. Solomon finally decided that the only way to find meaning and satisfaction in life is by giving God his proper place first of all.

Mankind is in the same struggle today, trying to find purpose, meaning, and satisfaction in life. Ecclesiastes teaches us that nothing can satisfy the empty human heart except the right relationship with God, which is only established when a person receives Jesus Christ into his life.

SONG OF SOLOMON

The Old Testament book called the Song of Solomon is the fifth book of Hebrew poetry in the Bible. Solomon wrote over 1000 songs, but this is the only one recorded in the Bible.

The Song of Solomon is a love poem which uses a description of the marriage union to give us a picture of the church's relationship to Jesus Christ.

The Song of Solomon shows how initial love of a man and a woman can grow, but may sometimes falter then continue on to mature love. Solomon shows us that God gives his approval to marriage and to love that grows. The Song of Solomon also teaches us that we should grow to maturity in our love for Jesus Christ, and look forward to the time when the church is presented to Jesus Christ just like a bride is presented to her groom at a wedding. The last book of the Bible describes the great wedding feast in heaven when this takes place.

This book should be read carefully as a practical guide for marriage today and as a reminder that God has invited us all to that great marriage feast in heaven.

ISAIAH

The Old Testament Book of Isaiah begins the writing of the prophets in the Bible. The word prophet refers to a person who speaks on behalf of another, just like when God told Moses that his brother Aaron would be his prophet or spokesman.

Non-predictive prophecy refers to declaring the truth on behalf of God, while predictive prophecy refers to declaring some future truth by the inspiration of God.

Isaiah was inspired of God to tell of the coming judgment on Judah because of idol worship. He even saw beyond the destruction and great captivity in Babylon to the future restoration of the nation.

Isaiah's prophecy also includes a detailed description of the crucifixion of Jesus Christ although written about 800 years before he came to earth

Another major theme of Isaiah is that God offers forgiveness, cleansing, mercy, and peace with God, but warns that if we reject these, then judgment will follow.

Isaiah also teaches us that even though our sins may be as glaring or red as scarlet, that God can make them white as snow and keep us in a state of peace with God. This book also reminds us that we can have forgiveness and peace with God when we accept his son Jesus Christ

JEREMIAH

The Old Testament Book of Jeremiah is a book of prophecy and mourning for the approaching judgment on the nation of Judah. Isaiah had warned the nation that unless they turned to God they would suffer, and now Jeremiah tells the people that judgment is at hand and there is no escape.

Jeremiah lived in an age much like today, when God's word was not popular. The people rejected the message as well as the messenger. Jeremiah was so discouraged that he said he would not even mention God anymore, and become known as the weeping prophet.

However, God had chosen Jeremiah to preach before he was born, and he said that God's word was like a fire burning inside him and he could not stop preaching.

Jeremiah was also inspired to write about the coming Messiah, Jesus Christ, and his death on the cross. He even saw beyond that to the return of Jesus and the events at the end of time.

Jeremiah is a reminder to us today that we need to hear God's word in order to know his will for our lives. He also teaches us that to obey will bring the blessing of God, while sin will bring certain judgment. Just as Jeremiah was called to proclaim God's message, God still uses men and women to proclaim the good news of Jesus Christ in today's world.

LAMENTATIONS

The Old Testament Book of Lamentations was written by the prophet Jeremiah as he mourns for the fall of Jerusalem and the captivity of his people. The title refers to crying aloud or lamenting and the central message is that sin brings the judgment of God on nations as well as on individuals.

This book is made up of 5 poems and was read by the Jews on the anniversary of the destruction of Jerusalem.

Even though Lamentations demonstrates the anger of God, it also shows the love and mercy of God as Jeremiah saw hope in the future when Jerusalem and God's people would be restored, while Babylon would be conquered.

This book teaches us that there is a price to pay for rebelling against God, and there's no escape from his judgment. Lamentations also reminds us that even though we have all sinned, God sent his son to pay the penalty that we deserve. We should be broken hearted, like Jeremiah, over our own sins as well as those of our nation and urgently persuade people to seek God's forgiveness by faith in Jesus Christ.

EZEKIEL

Ezekiel is one of the major prophets of the Old Testament. He was taken captive by King Nebuchadnezzar at an early age and carried to Babylon where he became the prophet to the Jews in exile. Ezekiel was a priest as well as a prophet and used unusual symbols or visual aids to impress his message on the Hebrew people.

Half of the Book of Ezekiel tells of the coming destruction of Jerusalem, while the rest tells of the restoration of Israel and God's judgment on Israel's enemies. Ezekiel even tells of future events at the end of time when Christ's kingdom will be established.

The central theme of Ezekiel is stated several times, and that is, (*) "ye shall know that I am the Lord".

God called Ezekiel through a vision and spoke to him many times through other visions and demonstrations of God's power such as a whirlwind.

Ezekiel also teaches us that God has not forsaken Israel, but will continue to use that nation to carry out his plan of salvation for mankind.

Ezekiel reminds us that while God used to speak to man through the prophets, he has spoken to us through his son Jesus Christ when he came to earth, and God continues to speak to us today through his word, the Bible.

(*) Ezek. 6:7

DANIEL

The Old Testament Book of Daniel records the history of God's people while in exile in Babylon. Daniel was taken captive in Jerusalem when he was very young and carried to Babylon where he ministered in the Royal Court. Daniel was a prophet of God, and he arose to political power as well.

Daniel was permitted to see nations and events at the end of time, and his prophecy helps us understand the Book of Revelation. His central theme is that God rules in the affairs of men and nations.

Daniel was not only a major prophet, but was also an example of a godly person in politics. At an early age he decided to live for God even though he was far from home. He continued to pray to God even when it was outlawed. As a result he was thrown into the lion's den. Daniel's three Hebrew friends were thrown into a hot, fiery furnace because they would not bow down before an image, but God was with them and they were not harmed either.

These stories should encourage young people to live for God today. Daniel also reminds us that if we find ourselves in a difficult or dangerous situation, that God can deliver us. But, if God does not deliver us from the situation, he will be in it along with us.

HOSEA

The Old Testament Book of Hosea is a book of prophecy written by Hosea. He told of approaching judgment on Israel because of the sin of idol worship during the time when the nation was divided into Israel in the north and Judah in the south.

Hosea tells how his unfaithful wife left him, but God sent him to bring her back. Hosea's acts of patience, compassion, love, forgiveness, and buying back or redeeming his wife was a picture of God's seeking the return of Israel when the nation had turned away from God.

The central theme of Hosea is "return to God". Hosea also tells of God's future blessings on the nation of Israel when the people would again turn to God.

Hosea preached in a time when there was a lack of knowledge of God because of false prophets and priests, and immorality was open.

Hosea is a serious reminder to us today that if we have strayed away from God, we must return to him before judgment comes. It also teaches us that we must hear the word of God if we are to know the truth.

JOEL

The Old Testament Book of Joel is a small book of prophecy written by a man whose name means "Jehovah is God". Joel was a prophet to the nation of Judah prior to the great captivity in Babylon.

Joel's main message was about the day of the Lord, referring to the future time when there will be a great outpouring of God's wrath on the world before the kingdom of Christ is established.

Joel also told of the coming of the Holy Spirit in a new way. This was partly fulfilled on the New Testament Day of Pentecost when the Holy Spirit gave the church unusual power to proclaim the good news of salvation by faith in Jesus Christ.

Joel also told of Israel's future restoration and God's judgment on the other nations.

Even though the events at the end of time may appear frightening, Joel gives us assurance that God will protect his people who trust in him. Joel also gives us confidence, like Paul in the New Testament that whosoever calls on the Lord will be saved from the penalty of sin.

AMOS

The Old Testament Book of Amos was written by a shepherd who was called by God to prophesy primarily to the nation of Israel.

The central message of Amos is (*) "Can two walk together, except they be agreed?" referring to the nations walking with God.

Amos told of approaching judgment on the surrounding nations because of their cruelty and oppression of Israel. He also told of God's judgment on Judah for despising God's law and against Israel for immorality.

However, Amos also saw beyond judgment to the time when Israel would again be established. He used several types or figures of speech to illustrate his message, saying that God would use a plumb line in Israel to show how far they had gone astray.

The Book of Amos is a reminder to us that it is a serious matter with God to oppress his chosen nation Israel. Amos also teaches us that sin brings the judgment of God, while repentance and obedience will give us his blessings.

(*) Amos 3:3

OBADIAH

Obadiah is the shortest book in the Old Testament. Obadiah means "servant of Jehovah", and Obadiah was God's messenger to the nation of Israel.

The people of Edom were descendents of Esau, the twin brother of Jacob, whose name was changed to Israel. The Edomites had a bitter hatred for Israel and refused to let the people of Israel pass through their land when traveling from Egypt to the Promised Land.

Because of Edom's sin against Israel, God pronounced judgment on them, and Obadiah gave them the message that (*) "as thou hast done, it shall be done unto thee", and Edom disappeared as a nation before the time of Christ. Obadiah also declared the blessing of God on the nation of Israel as his chosen people.

This little book encourages us to be a servant of God, for God is still looking for men and women that he can use. We are also reminded that God's protection and mercy are still on his people. We can call on God if we are in a difficult situation and find mercy and help today.

(*) Obadiah 1:15

JONAH

The Old Testament Book of Jonah contains one of the best known stories of the Bible. Jonah is a good example of God working through a man even though he was disobedient.

Jonah was called by God to go preach to the wicked city of Nineveh. Instead of doing what God wanted, Jonah tried to go in the opposite direction on a ship headed for Tarsish. God had to send a frightening storm at sea, and had Jonah thrown overboard so that a specially prepared fish could swallow him.

While in the fish Jonah changed his mind and prayed to God. God heard his prayer and gave him a second chance as the fish let him go on the land.

Jonah then obeyed God by preaching in Nineveh, where thousands of people believed in God and repented. However, Jonah was not pleased because he wanted to see God's wrath on these people. God had to teach Jonah another lesson, showing him that he did not have compassion for other people.

Jonah teaches us many lessons, but most of all he is a type of Christ, who spent three days in the grave before coming forth with the good news of salvation by faith in Jesus Christ.

MICAH

The Old Testament Book of Micah was written by a prophet whose name means "who is like Jehovah?" Micah was a prophet primarily to Judah, but he often included Israel as well. Micah's message is that judgment is at hand, but that God has promised future blessings. He told of the approaching invasion of Judah, the fall of Jerusalem, and the great captivity in Babylon.

Although this was a stern message, Micah also gave the Hebrew people hope, for he told of the future restoration of Israel, events at the end of time, and even told the place of Christ's birthplace at Bethlehem.

Micah's message is still a message of hope today, for he teaches us that God will forgive and forget our sins. As Micah urged the Hebrew people to accept God's offer to repent and live for him, we know that God makes the same offer today.

We also receive hope from Micah for he tells us that Christ's kingdom will some day be established, and God's people will have his bessings forever.

NAHUM

The Old Testament Book of Nahum was a short prophecy written by a man whose name means "comfort". Nahum wrote about the destruction of the city of Nineveh, the capital of Assyria, about 150 years after Jonah went there to preach.

Nahum's central message is like Jonah's, which was that judgment is at hand because of your great wickedness. Although there had been a religious revival in Nineveh after Jonah's preaching, the city had now gone deeper into sin than ever before.

Nahum's prophecy came true in 608 B.C. when the city of Nineveh was so completely destroyed, that shortly after the time of Christ the location of the city's ruins was uncertain.

While Nahum's message was on judgment, he also gave comfort to God's people by showing that God will punish the guilty who oppress the innocent.

Nahum reminds us today that each generation must encourage the next to remain true to God. He also reminds us that although God punishes sin, he has provided a substitute by letting his son Jesus Christ pay the penalty for the sins of all those who will accept him.

HABAKKUK

The Old Testament Book of Habakkuk is a prophecy about judgment on the city of Babylon. While Obadiah told of the judgment on Edom, and Nahum spoke of judgment on Assyria, now Habakkuk tells of the destruction of that city that became known as a symbol of the enemy of God's people.

The first part of the book contains a conversation between Habakkuk and God, while the second part describes an appearance of God. Habakkuk asks God how long sin would go on unpunished in wicked Babylon. God answers that he should wait and see what God will do, telling Habakkuk that (*) "the just shall live by his faith". Habakkuk also praises God for his past works and describes the joy of salvation.

Habakkuk is a powerful reminder to us today that sin will be punished, as none can escape God's judgment. We are also reminded that we can take our burdens or worries to God in prayer and leave matters in his hands with full confidence that God is in charge and can work things out somehow.

(*) Hab. 2:4

ZEPHANIAH

The Old Testament Book of Zephaniah was written by one of the prophets of Judah during the time when Jeremiah was also a prophet. Zephaniah told of coming judgment on Judah because of continued idol worship, but like the other prophets he also told of the future deliverance of God's people.

Zephaniah also told of God's wrath on the nations surrounding Judah who had oppressed God's people. However, he says that God's wrath will be great against Judah also because that nation had the advantage of hearing God's word.

Zephaniah even looks to the end of time when Christ's kingdom will be established and God's people will no longer be oppressed. This book has an important message for us as it reminds us that God expects more from people who have had the opportunity of hearing his word.

He also shows us that although God's people may have to be corrected or chastened, there will be a time of deliverance and healing. Zephaniah also reminds us that we can trust God with our lives while we wait for the return of Jesus Christ.

HAGGAI

The Old Testament Book of Haggai was written by a prophet whose name means "festive or happy". He was born in Babylon during the time of the great captivity of Israel. Haggai returned to Jerusalem with the first group that was sent back to rebuild the temple and the city.

The group that had returned was neglecting the building of God's temple and were only concerned about building their own houses. Haggai was sent with the message from God that it was time to consider their ways and build the house of God.

Haggai also gave the people a happy message of encouragement as he reminded the people that God had made a covenant with his nation Israel, and God would not forsake them. He also told of the future events at the end of time when God would shake up the Gentile nations, as the kingdom of Christ would be established.

Haggai's message is a timely reminder to us today that we need to consider our ways and get concerned about doing God's work. God has given us the task of preaching the good news of Jesus Christ to the whole world, and we must not get so busy with the things of the world that we don't have time to do the things of God which last for all eternity.

ZECHARIAH

The Old Testament Book of Zechariah was written after the return of God's people from the great captivity in Babylon. Zechariah was a prophet and priest and wrote more about the messiah, Jesus Christ, than any other prophet except Isaiah.

Zechariah's main theme was that God was jealous for his people and would punish those nations that oppressed them. He wrote of the rejection of Christ by Israel, but saw beyond that to his second coming when his kingdom will be established. Zechariah wrote specific details such as Christ's hands being pierced and God judging the nations in the valley of Armageddon.

Zechariah's writings should encourage Christians of all generations by reminding us of the return of Jesus Christ when the nations will be judged and Christ's kingdom will be established. We must remember the urgency of pressing people into the kingdom of God by preaching the gospel of Jesus Christ to every nation and language.

MALACHI

The Old Testament closes with the Book of Malachi which was written by a prophet whose name means "my messenger". After Malachi there will be 400 years of silence, when man did not hear from God until John the Baptist would come preaching in the wilderness.

The central message of Malachi is that the Messiah shall come. Malachi said that God's love had been demonstrated to his people, yet the love of God had been rejected. The people and prophets had rejected God's love by giving God inferior offerings, by cheating each other, intermarrying with heathen, by immorality, by robbing God through tithes and offerings, and by speaking against God.

Malachi shows again that God's' love is proven by sending his son to earth, and by remembering his people.

Malachi lived in a time much like today, when people reject the love and mercy of God and do not want to remember that God will hold us accountable for what we do while waiting for the return of his son, Jesus Christ.

THE 400 SILENT YEARS

There were almost 400 years between the closing of the Old Testament and the beginning of the New Testament. Although the world did not receive any new revelation from God during this time, this was still a very important political and religious era for Israel.

The Temple in Jerusalem had been rebuilt and worship of God restored, but most of the Jewish people had remained in the land of the great captivity. The remnant that returned were waiting for the Messiah to come and establish his kingdom.

The Chaldean Empire of Babylon was conquered by the Persians who then fell to Alexander the Great as the Greek Empire was established. The Greek Empire eroded away as the Roman Empire came, just as Daniel had predicted. Judah was a Roman province at the beginning of the New Testament.

During this time the religion of the Jews changed also. The oral traditions and laws were written into the Talmud which is still used by Jews today. This body of traditions was often referred to by Jesus.

Religious groups such as Scribes, Pharisees, and Sadducees came into existence with the ruling council called the Sanhedrin. It was this council that was responsible for the crucifixion of Christ.

During these 400 years God was setting the stage for the great appearance of his son Jesus Christ. God was still ruling in the affairs of men and nations just as he is today while we wait for the return of Jesus.

THE NEW TESTAMENT

The Bible is divided into the Old Testament which is centered in the Law of Moses, and the New Testament which is centered in the grace of God. The word testament means covenant or agreement and refers to God's agreements with mankind.

The Old Testament shows the sinfulness of man and his need for a saviour. The New Testament shows that God provided a saviour for mankind when Jesus came to earth as a human being.

The Old Testament requires judgment or penalty because of man's sins, while the New Testament gives the good news that God accepted the death of Jesus as sufficient penalty or payment for our sins. Throughout the New Testament we see the fulfillment of the Old Testament.

As we begin our study of the books of the New Testament we need to remember that Jesus Christ is the theme of every book in the Bible, but the New Testament gives us a much more complete revelation of him. The New Testament also gives us examples and principles to help us live the Christian life in today's confused world.

MATTHEW

The first book of the New Testament is the gospel according to Matthew. This account of the life and ministry of Jesus was written by Matthew the Jew who became a tax collector for the Romans. He became a disciple or follower of Jesus and later became an apostle, or one who is sent out with a message.

Matthew wrote primarily for the Hebrew people as he presented the New Testament as fulfilling the Old Testament promises of God to send the Messiah to be the King of Israel. Matthew records the ministry of Jesus in Galilee and Judea, including many miracles and his teachings such as the sermon on the mountain.

He presents Jesus as the king who was rejected by his people as he is crucified. Matthew also shows that Jesus is the king when he was resurrected after 3 days in the grave.

In Matthew we see the beginning of the church as the called out or separated people of God. Matthew's gospel ends with the final instructions of Jesus to the church, when he said to go into all the world and make disciples from all nations.

Matthew reminds us that the church has the same command in this generation, and the most urgent task of the church is to get the gospel to the whole world.

MARK

The New Testament Book of Mark is the story of Jesus Christ through the eyes of John Mark, who wrote primarily for the Roman mind. While Matthew pictured Jesus as the king, Mark presents him as a servant. He emphasizes the works or actions of Jesus which proved who he is.

Mark's central message is that Jesus came to minister to the people and to give his life as a ransom for them.

Throughout the book Mark refers to the cross. While he doesn't give the same details as the other gospel writers, he does give the resurrection of Jesus as a fact. He also records the final instructions of Jesus to the church to preach the gospel to every creature.

The concise, direct style of Mark is a good reminder to the scientific, precise world of today, that the gospel message of Mark is still true as Jesus Christ will still save anyone who will call on him.

LUKE

The gospel according to Luke is the New Testament's third book to give the story of the life and ministry of Jesus Christ. Luke gives special emphasis to the humanity of Jesus by referring to him as the son of man. Luke, who was a physician, writes especially for the intellectual Greek minds of his day.

The central theme of Luke is that Jesus came to seek and to save that which was lost.

Luke's account of the early life of Jesus is not included in the other gospels, and the story of the birth of Jesus at Bethlehem is one of the best known passages of the New Testament. Luke's gospel also shows the completely human nature of Christ as he was dependent on prayer. Throughout the Galilean and Judean ministry of Jesus, Luke records the human feelings that Jesus experienced.

The Gospel of Luke should remind us today that Jesus does understand our feelings, our fears, our weaknesses, and sins. Luke should make us appreciate more than ever what Jesus did for us when he suffered on the cross so that we can be forgiven for all our sins by accepting him.

JOHN

The Gospel of John is the fourth book of the New Testament to tell the life and ministry of Jesus while on earth. John, who also wrote the Revelation and three of the letters recorded in the Bible, presents Jesus as the son of God. His message was not directed toward just one nation, but is for all nations of the world and is referred to as the gospel of belief.

John's gospel also shows that although Jesus came to earth as human, he also had a divine nature as he is the son of God. The main theme of John is that (*) "as many as received him, to them gave he power to become the sons of God". This gospel was also written to convince people to believe in Jesus. It is the book so often used by missionaries to present the gospel to those who have never heard it before.

The miracles recorded by John also prove that Jesus is the son of God. The story of Jesus walking on the water is one of the best known in the Bible.

John also explains that a new birth is necessary in order to enter the family of God. He also teaches that the Holy Spirit's work is to glorify Jesus and not the Holy Spirit. John should remind us today that we can still become a part of the family of God when we believe in his Son Jesus Christ, and trust him to save us.

(*) John 1:12

ACTS

The New Testament Book of Acts was written by the physician Luke who also wrote one of the accounts of the life and ministry of Jesus. The Book of Acts gives the history of the early church as the good news of Jesus begins to spread throughout the world. The book might have been called the Acts of the Holy Spirit because it was the Holy Spirit that directed the early church and gave it power.

The first part of the book centers around the church at Jerusalem, Judea, and Samaria, while the second part focuses on Antioch and the regions beyond including western Europe. The principle person of the first part is Peter, while the second part follows the ministry of Paul.

The Book of Acts gives the message as well as the methods for taking the plan of salvation to a needy world. The Acts show the rapid growth of the church as the Holy Spirit gave the believers power to be witnesses of what they had seen and heard about Jesus.

This exciting book should remind the church of today that we still have the same command of taking the good news to every nation and language in the world. We should also remember that the Holy Spirit is still the source of power to convince the people of the world that (*) "whosoever shall call upon the name of the Lord shall be saved".

(*) Rom 10:13

ROMANS

The New Testament Book of Romans is a letter that Paul wrote to the Christians in the church at Rome prior to his arriving there. When Paul wrote this letter, the gospel had been preached in the Roman Empire for about 25 years and many churches had come into existence. These churches like the one at Rome had many questions concerning the gospel and how the gospel related to the nation of Israel. Paul was writing to answer these questions and to further explain Christianity.

The central theme of this letter to the Romans is that everyone has sinned against God, but that everyone can be saved from the penalty of sin by faith in Jesus Christ. This letter is often used by missionaries to explain how the gospel saves and how it affects the life of believers.

This letter shows the difference in what we are, and what we can become with God's help. Paul tells of his own struggle to overcome the power of sin, finally realizing that victory is through Jesus Christ.

This book should be studied carefully by all Christians today. It will make us appreciate what Jesus did for us when he died on the cross, and helps us to understand that hearing God's word will increase our faith in him.

1 CORINTHIANS

The New Testament Book of 1 Corinthians is a letter that Paul wrote in answer to a letter he had received. He was writing to the church at Corinth to correct problems and to help them live the Christian life in a wicked city. Corinth was known for its wealth, luxury and sin, and the church was being influenced.

The church also had internal conflicts which divided it into several groups, and Paul urged them to unite to exalt Jesus Christ and not man.

The central message of this letter is that the wisdom of man is not enough, and the church needs the wisdom of God. Paul also explains that God chose preaching as a way to give his word to the world.

This letter also answers questions on marriage and divorce, spiritual gifts that God gives, and gives advice that is still needed today for Christian living.

The first letter to the Corinthians should remind us that science and technology of today cannot answer spiritual questions, but God's word can. This letter also gives practical principles that help Christians live for God in today's wicked world.

2 CORINTHIANS

The New Testament Book of 2 Corinthians is Paul's second letter to the church at Corinth. In this letter Paul tells more of his personal hardships and suffering than in any of his other writings. His central message is that there is comfort from God for whatever our situation may be.

One of the titles of the Holy Spirit is the Comforter, and Paul explains the works of the Holy Spirit. Paul also encourages the church to be forgiving of those who have sinned, but repented, and to be separated from the evil of the world.

This letter also gives instructions for giving, for facing the grief of death, and for preparing for God's judgment of our works. Paul also defends his right to be an apostle.

This letter gives hope to those believers who may have been struggling with some sin by explaining that when a person accepts Christ he will become a new person who can overcome.

This letter is a powerful message of hope to people who want to become Christians but are afraid they can't live up to the standards of the Bible. Paul gives us the assurance that with God's help and with the Holy Spirit living in us, we can live victorious lives.

GALATIANS

The New Testament Book of Galatians is a letter from Paul to the church at Galatia, written to preserve the true gospel. This church was being influenced to change the gospel by adding some parts of the Law of Moses as a requirement for forgiveness of sin.

Paul's main message to the Galatians church is that they had been freed from the requirements of the law when Christ died on the cross. He further explains that a person is justified or considered forgiven by faith in Jesus Christ and not by any additional good deeds or laws.

This letter also teaches that the fleshly or human nature of man tends to all sorts of evil, while the person who receives Christ will find the Holy Spirit producing good fruit or results in his life.

Paul's letter is a timely reminder to the Christian world today that we must always be alert to new trends and so called new revelations, or prophecies that would change the simplicity of the gospel of faith in Jesus Christ.

EPHESIANS

The New Testament Book of Ephesians is a letter that Paul wrote to the church at Ephesus while he was a prisoner in Rome. Paul had spent two years building up the people of the church, and now he is writing to them about the many spiritual blessings that Christians enjoy.

Paul describes the heavenly call to the saints or believers to live up to God's standards of conduct. He explains that when a person accepts Christ he receives a new relationship with God, his citizenship is in heaven not the earth, and he becomes spiritually alive.

Paul also gives some practical advice for living the Christian life and for overcoming sin.

This letter shows that a person becomes a Christian by faith in Jesus Christ and not by doing good deeds. He also explains that Christianity is for people of all nations, languages, and social levels. Paul reminds the church that every believer is given some spiritual gift or ability that is to be used in building the church.

This letter should remind us to praise God for all that he has given us, and give us a greater desire to be involved in persuading people to receive Jesus Christ.

PHILIPPIANS

The New Testament Book of Philippians is another letter from Paul while he was in prison in Rome. He was writing to the church at Philippi, which was the first European city to have received the gospel of Jesus Christ.

Even though Paul was in prison, he was writing about the joy that he had through Jesus Christ. He explains that his purpose or goal of life was to live for Christ.

Paul explains that Christ, not man, should be the pattern for our conduct, our desires, our interest, our feelings, and even our thoughts, as he says we should have the mind of Christ. He encourages the church to rejoice and not complain or worry because God has promised to supply our needs. This letter has been referred to as God's psychology book as there are 19 references to the mind and correct thinking.

This letter should be read and studied carefully today as people try to cope with the pressures of life. We need to have the peace of God in our lives and Paul says that we can if we learn to control our thoughts.

While this may sound impossible, Paul says that all things are possible through Jesus Christ who gives us strength when we receive him.

COLOSSIANS

The New Testament Book of Colossians is Paul's third letter to a church while he was in prison in Rome. In this letter to the Christians at Colosse Paul presents Jesus Christ as the preeminent person in the church since Christ has all the attributes of God.

Paul encourages the Colossian church to be filled with the knowledge of Christ and to live godly lives. He shows that philosophy and religious systems of man are not enough, but that each person must personally know Jesus Christ through the experience of receiving him

Paul's letter also encourages the believers to put their affections and interest on the things of God more than on the things of the world. He again gives practical guides for the believer's relationship to each other, including the home relationships of husbands and wives and children.

Paul's letter is appropriate for today when too much emphasis is placed on our material possessions and not enough emphasis is given to spiritual matters.

We also need to be reminded by Paul's letter that Jesus Christ is still the head of the church and is to be worshipped and exalted above everything else.

1 THESSALONIANS

The New Testament Book of 1 Thessalonians is a letter that Paul wrote to the church at Thessalonica. Paul had preached there while on his second missionary trip but was forced to leave by the unbelieving Jews. Timothy later went to minister to the church and Paul wrote this letter after his return.

Paul wrote to the young church to explain the teaching of Christianity on such doctrines as the election of believers, the work of the Holy Spirit, and the second coming of Jesus Christ. This letter contains a long list of practical advice for daily living as Paul warns the believers of approaching persecution, but gives them hope by assuring them of the return of Christ.

Paul describes the return of Christ as being at a time that is least expected like a thief in the night, and therefore he warns the believers to be ready for his return at all times.

Paul also gives a list of 22 commands for Christians, including comforting one another, being patient, rejoicing, praying, avoiding the appearance of evil, and holding onto the things that are good.

This letter should remind us today to be ready for the sudden return of Christ by first of all receiving him, and then by living a life that is pleasing to him.

2 THESSALONIANS

The New Testament Book of 2 Thessalonians is Paul's second letter to the church at Thessalonica. This letter was written to correct some misunderstandings of his first letter, and to encourage the believers to stand fast and not give up under extreme persecution.

Paul reminds the church that God will judge the wicked who persecute the church and their suffering will someday come to an end. He warns the believers that before the Lord's return there will be a general falling away of many from the church and the man of sin, also known as the anti-Christ, will deceive many with false doctrines and great power.

This letter also gives practical advice for living while waiting for the return of Jesus. He warns the believers to mind their own business and not associate with disorderly people. He also established the principle that those who will not work should not eat.

Through all these warnings and commands Paul still gives the church hope by assuring them that Christ will return and that God's faithful people will be rewarded.

This letter should give us hope today as we still wait for the return of Christ who loved us enough to come to earth and die for our sins so that we can live forever with him.

1 TIMOTHY

The New Testament Book of 1 Timothy is Paul's letter to Timothy who was ministering to the church at Ephesus. Timothy's name means "honored by God" and Paul was writing to encourage him and to help him correct some false teachings in the church.

Paul's letter gives the qualifications for the elders or overseers of the church, and gives a charge or command, not only to the elders, but to the whole church to live by God's standards. Paul was not writing against women, but was trying to get the men to assume more leadership in the church.

Paul emphasizes the need to keep order in the church by preaching sound doctrine. He also gives some practical advice about prayer, the qualification for deacons, treatment of slaves, and caring for the needs of widows in the church.

Timothy had been taught the scriptures from childhood by his godly mother and grandmother, and Paul reminds Timothy of their influence on his life.

This letter to Timothy is still a valuable guide for how we ought to behave in the house of God. It is also a reminder that the influence of mothers and grandmothers can help children accept Christ at an early age.

This letter also reminds us that the best way to avoid the many false doctrines of today is by hearing the word of God, including the gospel of Jesus Christ.

2 TIMOTHY

The New Testament Book of 2 Timothy is Paul's second letter to Timothy while he was leading the church at Ephesus. Paul was writing while in prison and in this letter he reveals more of his personal joy than in any of his other letters. This is Paul's last letter as he was facing death soon.

Paul urges Timothy to preach sound doctrine, for in the last age there will be perilous times when many will fall away from true faith. He uses several figures of speech to describe the believers and the church, and warns them of persecution and great wickedness.

This letter also encourages Timothy as the pastor of the Ephesians church to be alert to false doctrines, using the inspired word of God to correct and instruct the people.

Paul's letter also includes his final, personal summary of his own life as he said that the time of his death was at hand. He had been faithful to finish the work that God had given him to do, and God would reward him.

This letter describes the spiritual condition of today's world and is a timely reminder to us to preach the word of God, and not be led into some form of religion that denies salvation by faith in Jesus Christ.

TITUS

The New Testament Book of Titus is Paul's letter to one of his Greek converts who had been a friend and fellow worker of Paul. Paul was writing to Titus to help him strengthen the church which had been established on the Island of Crete.

In this letter Paul stresses the importance of maintaining good works. He instructed Titus to appoint elders or overseers of each local church and give them the responsibility of leading that church.

Paul lists 14 qualifications for these elders and spells out their duties such as knowing God's word and convincing the people to believe it. He gives specific teachings for different age groups such as older men, older women, young people, and even servants.

Paul tells Titus that believers should obey the laws of the land, not speak evil of others, and always be ready to tell others of their faith in Christ.

This letter is a practical guide for churches today as it is important to not only have sound doctrine, but to maintain proper conduct as well.

As Paul's other letters teach, we must believe in Jesus Christ in order to get into heaven, while this letter shows the importance of maintaining good works while waiting to go there.

PHILEMON

The New Testament Book of Philemon is a short note or letter from Paul to his friend Philemon about a runaway slave named Onesimus. This slave had stolen from Philemon and run away to Rome where he met Paul in prison. Onesimus had become a Christian through Paul's influence, and now he wanted to make things right with his former master.

When Paul wrote to Philemon he asked him to accept Onesimus back as a slave, but also to accept him as a brother for Philemon was also a Christian.

In this letter Paul asks Philemon to charge what Onesimus had stolen to Paul's account saying that he would pay for the slave's debt. This action of Paul was a demonstration of Christ's paying for our sin debt by suffering and dying on the cross for us.

This letter also teaches us the value of an individual, whether master or slave, and reminds us to try to reach all levels of society with the good news that anyone can be saved by simple faith in Jesus Christ.

This letter to Philemon might also remind us of the importance of writing letters as a means of sharing our faith and encouraging others to accept Jesus Christ.

HEBREWS

The New Testament Book of Hebrews is a long letter written to the Hebrew people. While the author is uncertain, much evidence points to the apostle Paul or the physician Luke as the writer. However, the message of Hebrews is clear, and that is that there is no more sacrifice for sin as Jesus fulfilled all the demands of the law when he died on the cross.

The writer explains that Jesus is superior to all other beings including the angels, that the new covenant between God and man is superior to the old, and that the Christian life is superior to the life apart from God.

This letter gives the believer the assurance of being able to pray directly to God, and that our great high priest Jesus Christ also speaks to the Father on our behalf. Hebrews also tells us we have a promised land called heaven, and warns of the danger of letting sin harden our hearts so that we no longer believe in God.

A careful reading of this letter to the Hebrews should cause every Christian to thank God for all that we receive when Christ comes into our lives and should cause others to see their need of accepting Jesus Christ.

JAMES

The New Testament Book of James was one of the earliest letters of the early church. It is sometimes called the Proverbs of the New Testament because of its practical applications for everyday living. James the author, who was the brother of Jesus, was among the believers in the upper room after the resurrection of Jesus, and he later became pastor of the church in Jerusalem.

James was writing to the Hebrew Christians who were scattered abroad. He seems to contradict the writings of Paul, especially in regard to salvation being by faith instead of by good works. However, a close study of James shows that the two writers compliment each other as Paul says we are justified or right with God by faith, while James says we are justified for good works after we have faith in Christ.

The central thought of James is that we are to be doers and not just hearers of the word of God. This letter is very practical as James tells us to pray for wisdom, endure temptation or trials, learn to control our temper, and says that religion means controlling our tongues. He also lists some of the rewards for submitting to God in life.

James's teaching about healing is also relevant for today as he says we should anoint with the oil, including medicine that is available, then pray for God's help.

James's letter is a reminder that we all need God's help in life, and we can have it when we accept his son Jesus Christ.

1 PETER

The New Testament Book of 1 Peter is a letter that Simon Peter wrote to the Jews who were scattered abroad. Simon was a fisherman along with his brother Andrew before Jesus called them to follow him. Jesus changed Simon's name to Cephus in the Aramaic language or Peter in the Greek, and is a name that means "little rock".

Peter has been called the apostle of hope as he wrote to strengthen the believers during a difficult time. His central theme is that Christians have a living hope through Jesus Christ.

Peter also gives the believers some encouragement to live the Christian life at home as well as at church. He also reminds the believers that Jesus suffered because of evil men, and that Christians can also expect to suffer. However, he assures the believers of the return of Jesus Christ and gives hope that God will take care of his own.

Peter's letter should remind us today that we too are hoping for the return of Jesus Christ and therefore we can endure whatever hardships or disappointments we must face in life. He also reminds us that we can put our cares or worries on the Lord, knowing that he does care for us.

2 PETER

The New Testament Book of 2 Peter is a short letter from Simon Peter to Christians in general. This is another very practical letter as Peter warns believers about being led astray by false teachers, while assuring them that God has given everything necessary for them to live the Christian life.

Peter says that believers can take on the divine nature of God by adding virtue, knowledge, self control, patience, godliness, kindness, and love. He says that by adding these to faith, the Christian will have greater assurance of salvation.

The letter warns believers to beware of doctrines and teachers that contradict the word of God, by reminding them that the scriptures were written by holy men of God who were writing under the inspiration of the Holy Spirit. Peter was writing to remind the believers that people would ridicule the return of Jesus Christ, which he says would be accompanied by a great noise and heat so intense that the natural elements would melt.

While this may seem frightening, Peter says that God does not want anyone to spend eternity separated from God, so he is giving everyone an opportunity to be saved by believing in his son Jesus Christ.

1 JOHN

The New Testament Book of 1 John is a letter written by the apostle John who also wrote the gospel of John and the Book of the Revelation. John was writing to the Christians in general to assure them that they can know for sure that they are saved from the penalty of sin and therefore, assured of going to heaven.

Over 30 times John says "we know" as he uses contrasts such as light and dark, the Holy Spirit and evil spirits, and good deeds verses evil deeds. He reminds the Christians that Christ is our advocate or attorney before God, and that God shows his love for us by letting us become his children.

John also warns the believers to not believe everything that appears good, but to put everything to the test of God's word.

This first letter of John also refers to love almost 30 times, and he says that another way to know we are saved is that we will love other Christians.

John's letter is still a reminder to Christians that according to the Bible we can know we have eternal life if we have asked Christ to forgive our sins and to be Lord of our lives.

2 JOHN

The New Testament Book of 2 John is the second letter by the same John who wrote one of the accounts of the life and ministry of Jesus, and also the Book of Revelation. This short note was written to a friend to encourage her to guard against false doctrines and to hold onto the true doctrine of salvation by faith in Jesus Christ.

John, who calls himself the elder, warns the friend that there were already deceivers in the churches who were denying that Jesus had come to earth as a human. He says that true believers should not let such a person come into their homes to teach their false doctrines. He further says that believers should not even wish them God speed, or good luck as we might say today.

This letter of John should remind us today of the importance of continuing in the true gospel of Jesus Christ because there is so much religious confusion in the world.

John's statement is still true that a person does not have God in his life if he does not have his son Jesus Christ.

3 JOHN

The New Testament Book of 3 John is the third letter from the apostle John who wrote one of the gospels and the Book of Revelation. This very brief letter or note was directed to Gaius who was a source of joy for John. John also refers to Diotrephes who was hindering the spread of the gospel for selfish reasons, and to Demetrius, who had a good reputation among the believers.

Gaius is described as walking in the truth, being faithful to his responsibilities, and being known for his love for others.

Diotrephes, however, is described as wanting the preeminence or prominent place in the church. He would not receive John and had made malicious statements against him. Diotrephes would not host visiting missionaries and kept others from receiving them into their homes as well.

The third person, Demetrius, who was a Greek convert, had only good things said about him and he is a good example of Christian character.

This letter should remind us to help spread the good news of Jesus, like Gaius and Demetrius, and not be like Diotrephes whose selfish ambitions interfered with the work of others.

JUDE

The New Testament Book of Jude is a very short letter written by the brother of James to Christians in general. It is very similar to Peter's second letter in that Jude warns the believers against false teachers who were already present in the early church.

Jude says that these false teachers will slyly creep into the church and then begin to deny the Lord Jesus Christ. He compares them to the unbelieving Hebrews who were destroyed after escaping from slavery in Egypt, to the rebelling angels who were thrown out of heaven, and to the cities of Sodom and Gomorrah who were also destroyed because of their wicked ways.

Jude also says that these false teachers will be like Cain who wanted his own way, like Balaam by trying to make a profit from their doctrines, and like Korah who denied the authority of God's man.

This letter reminds Christians to fight to protect the true faith by praying, looking for the return of Jesus Christ, and by urging others to accept him as Lord.

Jude's letter is a solemn warning to Christians today to be alert to any new gospel or revelation that tries to change or add anything to the good news that Jesus died so that lost sinners can be saved.

REVELATION

(PART 1)

The New Testament Book of the Revelation was written by the apostle John who wrote the gospel of John and three short letters. The Revelation is the conclusion to the whole Bible and to history itself as John describes events at the end of time.

The word "revelation" means that which is uncovered or made known, and the Book of the Revelation makes known the events at the end of time when Jesus will return.

The Revelation came from God who gave it to Jesus Christ, who sent an angel to John with the message. John then wrote the message of the Revelation to seven churches of Asia. While the Revelation is difficult to understand, John promises a blessing to those who read and hear, and keep the things written in it.

The first part of the book describes the seven churches, commending them for good qualities, and challenging them to correct their errors. The first part reminds us that God is aware of the strengths and weaknesses of the churches and that churches of today can compare themselves to the churches of Asia.

Like every other book of the Bible, the Revelation is also about Jesus Christ and God's great plan for the salvation of mankind by faith.

REVELATION

(PART 2)

The second part of the Book of Revelation describes the events surrounding the return of Christ to earth when God's wrath will be poured out on the nations of the world. This part is more difficult to interpret as these events are still in the future and may not be clearly understood until they happen.

In this part Jesus is seen by John as the conquering, powerful King of Kings who comes to earth to establish his kingdom. Even though Satan and his angels resist, the outcome has already been determined, as believers from many nations and languages will reign with Christ.

The Revelation is an encouragement to Christians of every generation for it gives assurance that God will take care of his people. The Revelation also reminds us that the Bible closes with an invitation to all who are spiritually thirsty to come to Jesus Christ. The Revelation also gives a final warning against adding to or taking away anything from God's word. The same Jesus who is made known in the Revelation is still the son of God who will receive any sinner that will believe in him while waiting for these events at the end of time.

Printed in the United States
By Bookmasters